DEC 27 2018 DU

CONNECT WITH ELECTRICITY

HOW CONDUCTORS WORK

BY VICTORIA G. CHRISTENSEN

LERNER PUBLICATIONS ◆ MINNEAPOLIS

For my family, Bryan, Brooke, Jesse, and Claire.
Thanks for picking up the loose ends while I write.
—V.C.

Special thanks to content consultant Neal Clements, Adjunct Professor of Electrical and Computer Engineering, North Dakota State University

Lerner Publications Company
A division of Lerner Publishing Group, Inc.
241 First Avenue North
Minneapolis, MN USA 55401

For reading levels and more information, look up this title at www.lernerbooks.com.

Main body text set in Aptifer Slab LT Pro 12/18.
Typeface provided by Linotype AG.

Library of Congress Cataloging-in-Publication Data

Names: Christensen, Victoria G., author.
Title: How conductors work / by Victoria G. Christensen.
Description: Minneapolis : Lerner Publications, [2016] | Series: Connect with electricity | Audience: Ages 8–11. | Audience: Grades 4–6. | Includes bibliographical references and index.
Identifiers: LCCN 2015041873 | ISBN 9781512407822 (lb : alk. paper)
Subjects: LCSH: Electric conductors—Juvenile literature. | Electric insulators and insulation—Juvenile literature. | Semiconductors—Juvenile literature.
Classification: LCC TK3303 .C47 2016 | DDC 537.6/2—dc23

LC record available at http://lccn.loc.gov/2015041873

Manufactured in the United States of America
1-39354-21166-3/1/2016

CONTENTS

Lightning may strike a tree, building, or metal pole during a thunderstorm.

Thunderstorms are powerful. You have probably heard that it can be dangerous to stand next to a tree when out in a storm. Or maybe you've been warned not to hold a fishing rod or golf club during a storm. This is because every thunderstorm has lightning. Lightning looks for an easy path to the ground. This might mean a shorter path, like through a tall building. Or lightning might find an easy path through a conductor. A conductor is a material that allows electricity to flow through it. A tree, a fishing rod, a golf club—even water—can all be conductors. You can be a conductor too.

Many items can conduct electricity naturally and without human control, but engineers, scientists, and electricians also use conductors in their work. Electronic devices, electrical wiring, and machines we use every day have conductors. Whether we notice them or not, conductors are all around us.

CHAPTER ONE

SHOCKING ELECTRICITY

To understand conductors, you must understand a little about electricity. Electricity starts with the atom. An atom is a tiny bit of matter that's too small to see. It's the smallest unit that an element can be broken down to and still have the same characteristics of that element. Everything is made up of atoms. A group of atoms that are bound together is called a molecule. Your pets, your schoolbooks, and your teacher are made of atoms and molecules.

Atoms are made up of even smaller particles known as electrons, protons, and neutrons. The center of the atom, called the nucleus, contains the protons and neutrons. Electrons are attracted to the protons at the center, so they circle around the nucleus. Even though scientists cannot see these tiny parts of an atom, they have some theories about how they move. Think about the sun in the center of the solar system and the way the planets circle it. The electrons circle the center of the atom in a similar way. Most scientists think that electrons can also change their course and move closer or farther away from the nucleus.

AN ATOM

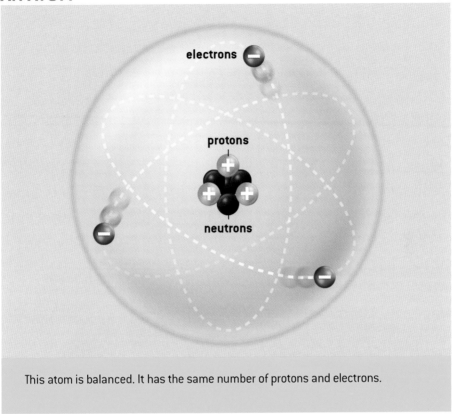

This atom is balanced. It has the same number of protons and electrons.

Electrons have a negative electrical charge, and protons have a positive charge. Neutrons are neutral—they have no charge. Atoms start out with the same number of electrons and protons, so the atom is balanced. When an atom loses an electron, it has more positive particles than negative particles. So the atom is positively charged. It is no longer balanced. Adding an electron to an atom makes a negative charge. A negatively charged atom is also unbalanced.

Electrons move about until they find a place on an unbalanced atom. A positively charged atom will attract a free electron to fill the space of a missing electron. Imagine playing musical chairs with nine chairs and ten kids. The music stops, and everyone finds a chair except for you and one other classmate. Only one chair is left. You both really want that chair and make a dash for it. Free electrons are like that too. They want to find a spot on an atom.

When electrons move from negatively charged parts of a wire to positively charged parts of a wire, electricity flows. We call the flow of electricity through a material an electric current. Some materials let electric current flow easily. These are called conductors.

Copper coils like these are often used in electric motors.

Resistance measures how a material reduces electric current that flows through it. Conductors have very low resistance.

Copper wire is a very good conductor. Most metals are good conductors. But copper is easy to find and inexpensive, so it's the conductor that is most often used in buildings and houses to carry the electricity we need to power our lamps, appliances, gaming consoles, and other electronic devices.

Electrical copper wires are often covered in rubber to protect engineers from the electric current that flows through the wires.

Materials that do not conduct electricity are called insulators, such as plastics, rubber, dry wood, and some other materials. Insulators have high resistance. Electrons in an insulator are held tightly inside an atom, so they're not free to move around like the electrons in a conductor. If a charge is transferred to one spot on an insulator, the charge will stay at that spot, because the molecules of the insulator do not allow the electrons to flow. So the charge doesn't spread through an insulator. Insulators can keep us safe from electricity.

Engineers use insulators to protect themselves and others from electrical shock. That's why copper wires are usually covered in rubber or plastic and why some tools have rubber handles.

Alessandro Volta was an Italian scientist, physicist, and chemist. He's considered to be a pioneer of electrical science.

Electricians use rubber boots, rubber gloves, and insulating hard hats. Rubber can stop electricity from shocking a person. Glass is also a good insulator. Power lines have glass or ceramic insulators to stop electricity from moving down the pole. Ceramic is made from clay and also is used inside some electrical equipment to separate conductors.

Conductors and insulators are both important to the study of electricity. Alessandro Volta (1745–1827) was the first scientist to make a list of conductors, called the electromotive series. Volta did experiments to measure the electrical effect of touching two different metals together. Although he did not understand how this worked, modern scientists know that some metals lose their electrons very easily. When two different metals touch, their electrons can move from one metal to the other, seeking balance. When the electrons move, this is a form of electricity.

Volta ranked a list of metals by how easily the metal atoms lose electrons. He described the difference between charges in two substances as their electromotive force, and we call this force voltage. Voltage describes the strength of the electrical force. Named after Volta, volts are the units we use to measure voltage.

VOLTA'S ELECTROMOTIVE SERIES
Zinc
Lead
Tin
Iron
Copper
Silver
Gold
Graphite
Manganese ore

The farther apart two metals are from each other on this list, the greater the voltage they produce when they make contact with each other. For example, zinc and graphite can produce more voltage than zinc and lead.

CHAPTER TWO

LIGHTNING STRIKES

Electricity can take two forms: dynamic and static. *Dynamic* means "constantly changing," and dynamic electricity is used in electronics and appliances. Lightning and sparks are forms of static electricity. When water molecules in clouds rub together, they cause a huge negative charge to build up. A charge is the amount of unbalanced electricity in an object, based on its number of electrons and protons. When lightning strikes, electrons in the negatively charged cloud zap down to the

FACTS ABOUT LIGHTNING

- Lightning can strike up to 10 miles (16 kilometers) away from any rain.
- A person who is struck by lightning does not have an electrical charge.
- Lightning can move up to 220,000 miles (354,056 km) per hour.

CHARGED THUNDERSTORM

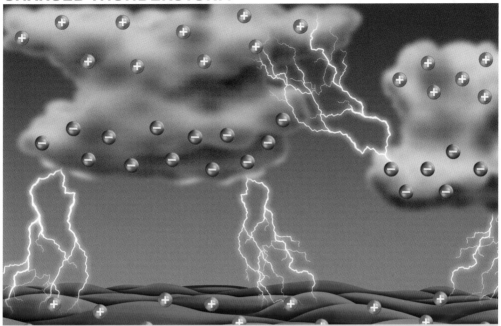

In a thunderstorm, negatively charged electrons in the clouds shoot down to the positively charged ground. This movement causes the bright branches of light that we know as lightning.

positively charged ground. This is like the shock you get when you drag your feet across the carpet and then touch a doorknob. You have a negative charge from the electrons you scraped off the carpet. These electrons then zap through the air to the positively charged doorknob and make a spark. Lightning is the same kind of electrical shock but on a much larger scale.

Lightning might take a short path to the ground through a tall building. During the 1920s and 1930s, companies were in a race to see which one could build the tallest skyscraper in New York City.

Builders even tried to trick one another. The architect of the Chrysler Building had a 185-foot (56-meter) spire secretly built inside the building. When the rest of the building was done, the workers quickly added the spire to the top. The Chrysler Building became the tallest building in the world. That didn't last for long though.

The builders of the Empire State Building had a 200-foot (61 m) spire built as well. When the spire was added, the Empire State Building became the tallest building in the world and held that rank for the next forty years. It is struck by lightning up to one hundred times a year.

An ironworker during the construction of the Empire State Building, with the Chrysler Building and its 185-foot (56 m) spire behind and to his left

Engineers can design buildings so they are safe during storms. They design metal lightning rods that provide a path for lightning to get to the positively charged ground instead of burning down the building or possibly harming the people inside. Designers included a lightning rod at the top of the Empire State Building, which made the building 1,454 feet (443 m) tall.

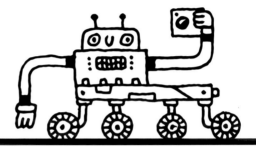

SOLVE IT!

FRANKLIN'S ELECTRIC KITE

In the eighteenth century, inventor Benjamin Franklin thought that lightning was a form of electricity and wanted to test his theory. He knew lightning often strikes tall buildings. But because no tall buildings were nearby, Franklin thought a kite would be a good way to get close to the clouds during a storm. The kite was made of a silk handkerchief, two sticks, and a string. But he also attached one more thing to the string: a key. Why did Franklin attach a key to his kite string? *(The answer key is on page 35.)*

CHAPTER THREE

WATER AS A CONDUCTOR

What is in the water that you drink? What is in the water in a lake or river? You've probably heard that water is also called H_2O. That means water molecules contain two hydrogen (H) atoms and one oxygen (O) atom. Water also contains dissolved minerals, such as salts. Without any dissolved minerals, water would not conduct electricity. But salts and many substances in water allow electrons to move more freely and allow the water to conduct electricity. Specific conductance measures how well water conducts electricity. Seawater is salt water and has high specific conductance.

It doesn't matter if the water is from the faucet, a lake, or a puddle. Water is a good conductor of electricity.

The dissolved minerals in the water that you drink make it a good conductor for electricity.

HUMAN LIGHTNING ROD

Humans are about 60 percent water. The brain, heart, lungs, and kidneys all need water to function. Even skin and bones contain water. Because people are mostly water, an electric current can pass through them. People can act as a conductor for electricity. A Shenandoah National Park (*right*) ranger named Roy Sullivan was struck by lightning seven separate times. He survived each time. Some people aren't as lucky.

It's dangerous to be in water when lightning might strike or when using an electric appliance. Electricity that flows through water in a lake or bathtub would flow through a person too.

The only type of water that doesn't conduct electricity is pure water. Pure water is water with no dissolved minerals or substances. Its specific conductance is about zero. But there isn't pure water in nature. The water in bathtubs and swimming pools isn't pure either. Distilled water and some water made for laboratories is pure. Since pure water will not conduct electricity, it is considered an insulator.

In school you might do experiments to see how water conducts electricity. In one experiment, a battery is connected to a lightbulb through a circuit, a closed path through which electricity can flow.

The dissolved minerals in salt water make it a good conductor for electricity. In this experiment, the water completes the circuit, allowing electrons to travel to the lightbulb and provide power to light it.

When all the wires are connected and there are no breaks, you have a completed circuit. But the circuit can also be completed if the wires are connected by a conductor like water. Two of the wires run from the battery and the lightbulb into a container of water. First, the wires are put into distilled water, but the light will not work. The second time, the wires are put into salt water. The light works!

In salt water, the dissolved salt releases free electrons. Remember that free electrons are always looking for a positively charged atom? Free electrons move from atom to atom in the water. This is what makes the water conduct electricity.

CHAPTER FOUR

METALS AND GRAPHITE

About 75 percent of all known elements are metals. Metals conduct electricity and heat very well. Why are metals such good conductors? All solids are made of atoms, but in metals, the atoms hold together in a very specific way. Imagine a loosely knit scarf. Air can move freely through all the holes in the scarf. The atomic structure in metals is similar. Some electrons remain free to move. They move throughout the whole material, just as air moves through a loosely knit scarf.

Metals are such good conductors that engineers use them in many of their designs. One example is an electric fence. Electric fences keep animals inside a yard or field.

Some farmers use electric fences like this one to keep their animals safe and secure.

FARADAY CAGES

Scientist Michael Faraday wanted to prove that while electrons collect on the outside of metal, the inside doesn't hold a charge. In 1836 he built a square cage, 12 feet (3 m) on each side, wrapped with copper wire and tinfoil. He applied an electric voltage to the cage to show that it didn't affect the inside. In one of his experiments,  he even climbed inside! But he was safe. The electrons rearranged around the cage's surface and created an electrically neutral area inside the cage. This is why passengers in a car or airplane are safe during a storm. The metal on the outside of the vehicle protects the inside.

These fences have a voltage applied to them that can shock an animal that touches it. This works because the animal completes an electrical circuit between the fence and the earth.

Copper is the most common conductor used by engineers. It occurs naturally in its pure form, so it is relatively easy and inexpensive to make into wire. Copper can conduct heat too. That's why it's used in some kitchen pans.

The metal that conducts electricity best is silver, followed by copper and then gold. You probably don't hear about silver conductors very often though. That's because copper is cheaper than silver and gold and is less likely to be damaged by chemical reactions.

THE EIFFEL TOWER—THE WORLD'S LARGEST LIGHTNING ROD?

The Eiffel Tower was the world's tallest structure from 1889 to 1930. More than fifteen thousand pieces of iron were used to build it. But iron is a good conductor for electricity. The tower is struck by lightning during most thunderstorms. To keep people safe, the Eiffel Tower was constructed with lightning rods in each corner. These were made from metal pipes buried 6 feet (1.8 m) deep at the base of the tower and rising to the top. Then a lightning strike can be carried safely to the ground through the lightning rod.

Silver can be damaged if it's exposed to certain elements. But silver is used as a conductor in special equipment, such as some satellites. It's covered with thin plating to protect it from being damaged.

Gold is a good conductor, but it's expensive. Small amounts of gold are used in many types of electronics though, such as cell phones, calculators, and global positioning system (GPS) devices. Around one billion cell phones are made every year, and it's possible that most of them contain about fifty cents' worth of gold!

Iron is a metal that is also a good conductor. Many lightning rods are made of iron.

Another material that can conduct electricity is graphite. It is a form of carbon and can be found in some rocks. It's the gray stuff inside your pencils. You might have heard someone use the term *lead pencil*, but this is only a myth. The core of the pencil is not made from lead but from graphite.

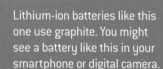

Lithium-ion batteries like this one use graphite. You might see a battery like this in your smartphone or digital camera.

BATTERY PACK

Li-ion

Graphite is the only nonmetal solid that is a conductor. It is a very strong yet very lightweight material. Graphite is commonly used for parts and machines in the steel industry. It's also used in brake linings and other parts of a car. Fishing poles are often made from graphite, which makes them dangerous to use during a thunderstorm. Some batteries use graphite because of its unique properties.

SOLVE IT!

LIGHTNING STRIKES

You know it is not a good idea to go outside in a thunderstorm. Between 2006 and 2013, 261 people in the United States were struck by lightning. Most of these people were enjoying outdoor activities, like fishing, camping, and golfing. A car can be a safe place to take shelter during a thunderstorm, but taking shelter in a golf cart is not a good idea. Why do you think that is? *(The answer key is on page 35.)*

CHAPTER FIVE

SEMICONDUCTORS

Materials that fall somewhere between conductors and insulators are called semiconductors. A semiconductor's conductivity, or ability to conduct electricity, increases with increasing temperature. This is opposite of the way metals behave. A metal's conductivity decreases with increasing temperature.

The electrons in an atom are in layers called shells. The electrons in the outer shell can form bonds with neighboring atoms. Most conductors have just one electron in the outer shell of their atoms, but semiconductors usually have four electrons in the outer shell. These four electrons can bind with electrons in other atoms. If these atoms are all made of the same substance, they can bind with one another in a very orderly way, like in crystals for example. Crystals have

Microprocessor chips are important parts in computers. These chips wouldn't be able to work without semiconductors.

atoms that are arranged in a pattern that is repeated throughout the material. The four electrons in the outer shell of the atom are bonded to the next atom, so the electrons are not free to move and conduct electricity.

Semiconductors differ from conductors in the way they are used. Engineers are able to change the conductivity of different areas of the semiconductor material moment to moment. This allows them to steer an electrical charge around computer chips. Engineers can easily control the conductivity and can operate semiconductors like a switch.

SEMICONDUCTOR ATOMS

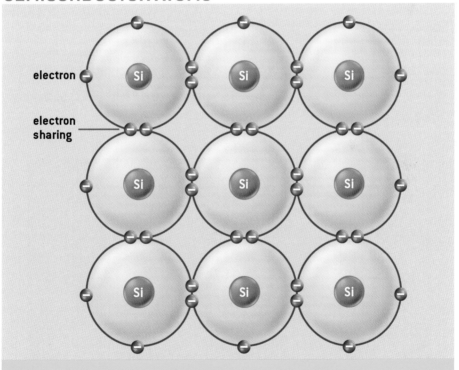

The atoms of semiconductors like silicon, for example, usually have four electrons on their outer shell. The atoms can easily bind together.

This is why semiconductors are used in many electronics like computers, radios, and microwaves.

Silicon is the most common semiconductor used in electronics. It's a crystal that is extracted from sand. Engineers can add an impurity, maybe a chemical like boron or arsenic, to pure silicon to increase its ability to conduct electricity.

SEMICONDUCTORS IN SPACE

Solar panels provide satellites with electricity. The solar panels on satellites need to be very large. Most solar panels are not very efficient, so many are needed to generate enough electricity to power a satellite. But some modern semiconductors are made from elements, like gallium arsenide, that are more efficient than silicon. Engineers are starting to use gallium arsenide in satellites. This material allows engineers to build smaller solar panels. Satellites are able to transmit signals around Earth in just seconds. They couldn't do this without semiconductors and solar panels.

A SOLAR CELL

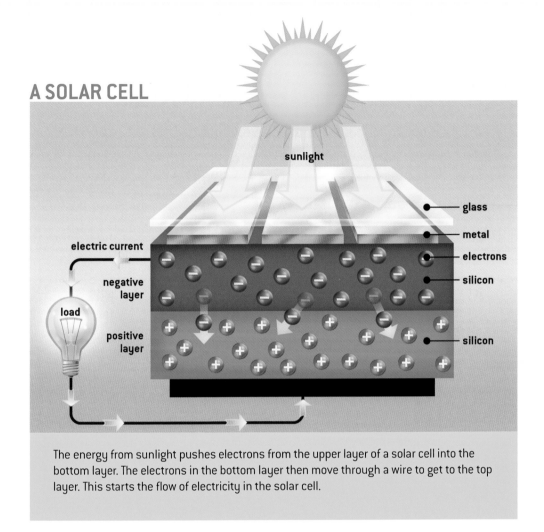

sunlight

glass

metal

electrons

silicon

silicon

electric current

negative layer

positive layer

load

The energy from sunlight pushes electrons from the upper layer of a solar cell into the bottom layer. The electrons in the bottom layer then move through a wire to get to the top layer. This starts the flow of electricity in the solar cell.

Silicon can also be used in solar cells, which make up a solar panel. Solar cells convert sunlight into electricity. Solar panels on houses, businesses, and farms use a free source of energy—the sun. A solar cell is made from two layers of silicon. The bottom layer has more protons than electrons, while the top layer has more electrons than protons. When the sun shines on the cell, the energy knocks the electrons from the top layer to the bottom layer.

This causes the electrons in the lower layer to move up through a wire to the top layer, creating a current and starting the flow of electricity. Solar cells can be used in calculators, homes, and many other devices.

One solar cell is enough to make a calculator work, but you would need many to provide electricity to a house. The solar panel on a house can have one hundred solar cells and a house might have dozens of panels. Solar cells create direct current (DC), where the current only travels in one direction, just like in a battery. But most houses use a different kind of current called alternating current (AC). With alternating current, the electric current is constantly changing directions. To power a house, the current from a solar cell has to be changed to alternating current. Solar cells use electrical devices called inverters to change the current from DC to AC.

The solar panels on solar farms work just like the solar panels on a house, but solar farms use many more panels. Solar farms also use semiconductors to generate electricity with solar panels, and can provide electricity for many houses and businesses.

CHAPTER SIX

SUPERCONDUCTORS

Some metals have no resistance to an electric current. Electricity flows through these metals very fast, without losing energy. These extremely low-resistance materials are called superconductors. They usually only conduct at very high or low temperatures and are not very common.

Resistance can change with temperature. Take tin, for example. A tin wire is a good conductor. It has low resistance. But if you heat it up, it has more resistance. Why? Because at a high temperature, the atoms inside tin are more active, so the electrons find it hard to flow. Imagine trying to run to the far end of a very busy mall.

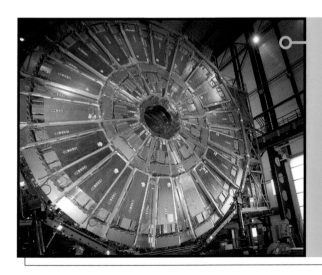

The world's largest superconducting magnet is used in the Large Hadron Collider. The Large Hadron Collider is the largest machine in the world, and it studies the universe's tiniest particles.

It would be difficult because of all the people you would have to dodge, just like electrons find it difficult to flow around other busy particles. But think about what might happen if you cool tin. The particles are less active, making it easier for the electrons to move through them and for electricity to flow. Think of how much easier it would be to run to the other end of a mall if everyone else stood still.

There are many theories about how superconductors work. Scientists are still learning about them. They are called superconductors because they have a "super" ability to "conduct." But conducting is not the only thing they can do. They are diamagnetic—they don't let magnetism enter them. How do they do it? Put a superconductor in a magnetic field. Electric currents will flow through the superconductor's surface and create another magnetic field. This magnetic field cancels the original field trying to get inside.

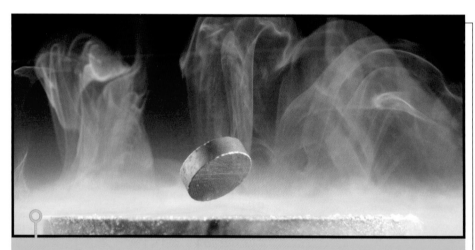

This ceramic cylinder (*bottom*) is a superconductor. Because it is diamagnetic, the magnet floats above it.

BULLET TRAINS

Superconductors are used for bullet trains. In Japan, bullet trains use an electric motor and go 200 miles (321 km) per hour. Train tracks in the United States have many curves, but bullet trains run on straight steel rails with very few turns. Bullet train tracks create magnetic fields near the rails. Superconductors and magnets lift and move train cars above the tracks so these trains seem to float over the rails. One bullet train traveled 340 miles (547 km) per hour!

Engineers use superconductors to design better motors, magnets, and wires. Superconducting wires can carry a lot of electricity. They carry much more electricity than copper wires of the same size. These superconducting wires can be used in magnets for scientific or medical equipment, like machines that show internal organs without surgery. These are called magnetic resonance imaging (MRI) machines. Conductors, insulators, semiconductors, and superconductors are all important to the study of

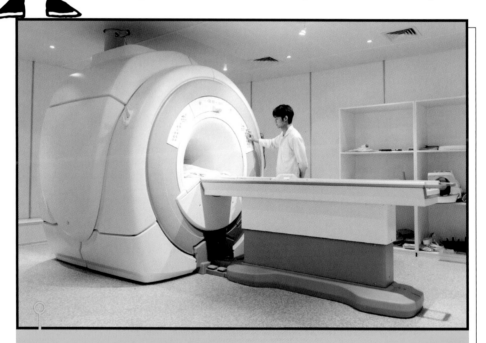

The superconducting wires in the magnets of an MRI machine allow it to locate atoms in our bodies. The atoms respond with their own magnetic field, which the MRI machine's magnets detect and use to create an image of the inside of a patient's body.

electricity. Scientists and engineers use some of these materials to design things we use every day, like televisions and cell phones. They also use these materials to design high-tech instruments that only scientists use. Scientists and engineers are still discovering new ways to use conductors, insulators, semiconductors, and superconductors for the future.

CONDUCTOR OR INSULATOR?

Your job is to find out which materials are conductors and which materials are insulators. Ask an adult for help with this experiment. This experiment uses low-voltage battery power. Never use high-voltage electricity from a household outlet.

WHAT YOU'LL NEED

- a writing utensil and paper
- two strips of copper wire
- a wire stripper
- a D cell battery
- a miniature lightbulb with a lightbulb holder (flashlight size)

- tape and paper clips
- a wire cutter
- items to test: an empty soda can, a plastic spoon, a metal spoon, a key, an apple, and other small items from your house or classroom

WHAT YOU'LL DO

1. First, make a two-column table on a sheet of paper to record your findings. The first column will list each item you test. In the second column, you will mark whether the item powered the lightbulb.
2. Make your circuit: strip the rubber or plastic from the ends of the wires with the wire stripper. Connect one end of each wire to the battery at its terminals. The terminals on a D cell battery are on each end. Connect the other end of each wire to the terminals on the bulb holder. The terminals are located on each side of the bulb. Use tape or paper clips to attach the wires to the terminals. At this point, the lightbulb should light up.
3. Next, cut one of the wires to break the circuit. Strip the two newly cut ends of wire. This is where you will test your items.
4. Touch each item (one at a time) with both wires. Did the lightbulb turn on? Note your findings in your chart. Continue checking items to see which complete the circuit and power the lightbulb. If the item is an insulator, the light will not work. If the item is a conductor, the light will work.

FOLLOW-UP

Which items were conductors, and which were insulators? Can you notice any similarities or differences between the conductors? What about the insulators?

FRANKLIN'S ELECTRIC KITE (PAGE 15)

Franklin attached a key to his kite string because keys are made from metal. Metal is a good conductor. Water is a good conductor too. So when lightning struck the key and traveled through the key and wet kite string, they conducted electricity.

LIGHTNING STRIKES (PAGE 23)

Cars are a safe place to be during a thunderstorm because they act like Faraday cages. The metal on the outside of the enclosed car keeps the people inside safe. A golf cart is not enclosed. There are no doors. The people inside a golf cart might be out of the rain, but they are not protected from lightning.

GLOSSARY

atom: the smallest unit of any chemical or chemical element that still has the characteristics of that chemical or chemical element

chemical: a substance that is used in a reaction to change atoms or molecules

conductivity: a material's ability to conduct electricity (or heat)

electrical charge: the amount of unbalanced electricity in an object, linked to the number of electrons and protons. Objects can have positive and negative charges on their surface.

electrical force: the difference between charges in two substances

electric current: the passing of electricity through a wire

electron: the part of an atom with a negative electrical charge. Electrons move around an atom's core.

energy: power that comes from electricity, heat, or other sources. Energy can be stored in a battery and can produce light, heat, or motion.

insulator: material that doesn't easily give up electrons. This limits the flow of current.

specific conductance: a measure of how well water can conduct an electric current

volt: a unit of electrical force. It measures how strongly an electric current is sent around an electrical system.

SELECTED BIBLIOGRAPHY

Brain, Marshall. *The Engineering Book: From the Catapult to the Curiosity River; 250 Milestones in the History of Engineering.* New York: Sterling, 2015.

Faraday, Michael. *Faraday's Experimental Researches in Electricity: Guide to a First Reading.* Edited by Howard J. Fisher. Santa Fe, NM: Green Lion, 2001.

Farndon, John. *1000 Facts on Science and Technology.* Great Bardfield, UK: Miles Kelly, 2001.

Franklin, Benjamin. *The Autobiography and Other Writings.* Edited by Kenneth Silverman. New York: Penguin, 1986.

Woodford, Chris, Luke Collins, Clint Witchalls, Ben Morgan, and James Flint. *Cool Stuff and How it Works.* New York: DK, 2005.

FURTHER INFORMATION

Energy Safe Kids
http://energysafekids.org/electric-safety/kids/electricity-basics/conductors-and
-insulators/
Check out this website to learn more of the basics about electricity.

Pegis, Jessica. *What Are Insulators and Conductors?* New York: Crabtree, 2012.
Explore the electrical properties of different materials.

Science Kids
http://www.sciencekids.co.nz/gamesactivities/circuitsconductors.html
Play a game about circuits and conductors!

Shea, C. O. *Conductors and Insulators.* New York: Gareth Stevens, 2013.
Find out more about currents, conductors, and insulators.

Thunderbolt Kids
http://www.thunderboltkids.co.za/Grade6/03-energy-and-change/chapter2.html
Learn more about experiments on conductors and insulators.

Walker, Sally M. *Investigating Electricity.* Minneapolis: Lerner Publications, 2012.
Discover more about how energy works through examples and fun experiments in
this exciting book about electricity.

INDEX

PHOTO ACKNOWLEDGMENTS

The images in this book are used with the permission of: © iStockphoto.com/Sashatigar (robots and electrical microschemes); © iStockphoto.com/da-vooda (electronic icon); © iStockphoto.com/alenaZ0509 (zigzag background); © iStockphoto.com/Kubkoo (color dots background); © iStockphoto.com/SVphotography, p. 4; Rob Schuster, pp. 7, 13, 25, 27; © Fireflyphoto/Dreamstime.com, p. 8; © leschnyhan/iStock/Thinkstock, p. 9; © Photos.com/Thinkstock, p. 10; © iStockphoto.com/Stefano Garau, p. 12; © Everett Collection Historical/Alamy, p. 14; © Georgios Kollidas/Dreamstime.com, p. 15; © iStockphoto.com/kedsanee, p. 16 (water glass); © David McSpadden/flickr.com (cc by 2.0), p. 17; © Charles D. Winters/Science Source, p. 18; © iStockphoto.com/Christian Colmer, p. 19; © GL Archive/Alamy, p. 20; © iStockphoto.com/Velishchuk, p. 21; © Aleksander Kovaltchuk/Dreamstime.com, p. 22; © iStockphoto.com/Krystian Nawrocki, p. 24; NASA/GSFC, p. 26; © AFP/Getty Images, p. 29; © Phil Degginger/Science Source, p. 30; © iStockphoto.com/Sean Pavone, p. 31; © iStockphoto.com/nimon_t, p. 32.

Cover: © Gabbro/Alamy (satellite); © iStockphoto.com/Kubkoo (color dots background); © iStockphoto.com/alenaZ0509 (zigzag background); © iStockphoto.com/Sashatigar (robots and electrical microschemes); © iStockphoto.com/da-vooda (electronic icon).